If you were an

Antonym

by Nancy Loewen
illustrated by Sara Gray

PICTURE WINDOW BOOKS
Minneapolis, Minnesota

antonym (ant) a word that has the opposite meaning of another word

Editors: Christianne Jones and Dodie Marie Miller
Designer: Tracy Davies
Page Production: Lori Bye
Art Director: Nathan Gassman
The illustrations in this book were created with acrylics.

Picture Window Books
A Capstone Imprint
1710 Roe Crest Drive
North Mankato, MN 56003
www.capstonepub.com

Library of Congress Cataloging-in-Publication Data
Loewen, Nancy, 1964-
If you were an antonym / by Nancy Loewen ; illustrated by Sara Gray.
p. cm. — (Word fun)
Includes bibliographical references and index.
ISBN-13: 978-1-4048-2384-6 (library binding)
ISBN-10: 1-4048-2384-0 (library binding)
ISBN-13: 978-1-4048-2388-4 (paperback)
ISBN -10: 1-4048-2388-3 (paperback)
1. English language—Synonyms and antonyms—Juvenile literature.
I. Gray, Sara, ill. II. Title.
PE1591.L65 2006
428.1—dc22   2006027310

Looking for antonyms?

Watch for the **big**, **colorful words** in the example sentences.

Special thanks to our advisers for their expertise:

Rosemary G. Palmer, Ph.D., Department of Literacy
College of Education, Boise State University

Susan Kesselring, M.A., Literacy Educator
Rosemount—Apple Valley—Eagan (Minnesota) School District

If you
were an
antonym ...

3

BIG
or
SMALL.

5

If you were an antonym, you would be a word that means the opposite of another word. Opposite means to be completely different from something else.

The room could be DARK or **LIGHT**.

You could be **HAPPY** or **SAD**.

If you were an antonym, you could be a complementary antonym. You would be all or nothing. You would either be one thing or the other.

Your dad's radio is either **ON** or **OFF**.

8

If you flip a coin, you get either **HEADS** or **TAILS**.

If you were an antonym, you could be a relational antonym. You would be in a pair with your opposite. You would have no meaning without your opposite.

In order to be a
STUDENT,
you must have a
TEACHER.

In order to be
a **PARENT**,
you must have
a **CHILD**.

If you were an antonym, you could be a graded antonym. You could show how words are related. EMPTY and FULL are antonyms, but between EMPTY and FULL are many possibilities.

The cookie jar might be HALF FULL or NEARLY EMPTY.

12

The cookie jar might be
ALMOST FULL or
MOSTLY EMPTY.

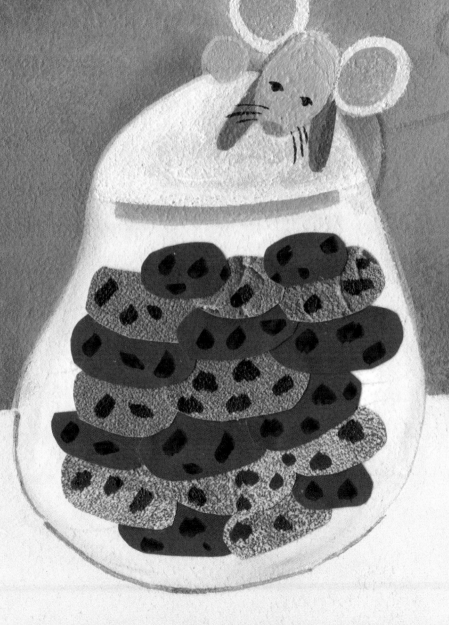

If you were an antonym, you could have a prefix. A prefix is added to the beginning of a word. Adding a prefix can completely change a word's meaning.

SENSE becomes

NONSENSE.

WIN
$ $ $ $

LUCKY becomes UNLUCKY.

WIN
$ $

15

If you were an antonym, you could have a suffix. A suffix is added to the end of a word. Adding a suffix can also change a word's meaning.

HOPEFUL becomes **HOPELESS.**

CAREFUL becomes CARELESS.

17

If you were an antonym, your opposite would be a synonym.
Synonyms are words that mean the same thing.

SICK and **ILL** are synonyms.
They mean the same thing.

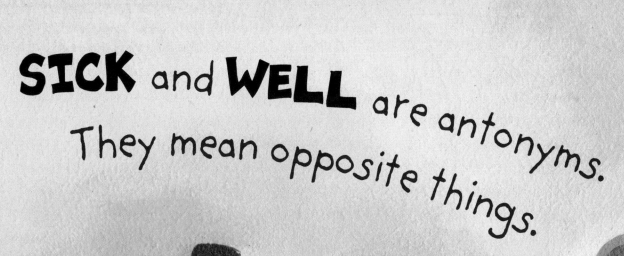

SICK and **WELL** are antonyms. They mean opposite things.

19

If you were an antonym, you could be an autoantonym. You would be a word that has two meanings that are opposite of each other.

A **BILL** can be a piece of paper money.

A **BILL** can also be a statement saying that you owe money.

You would always be an opposite ...

... if you were an antonym!

ANTONYM ANTICS

Cut out 30 squares of heavy paper. Next, write down 15 pairs of antonyms (one word on each square). Now, mix the cards up and place them face down on a flat surface. Take turns flipping over two cards. If the words are antonyms, you get to keep the pair and continue playing. If the cards aren't antonyms, flip them back over and move to the next player. When all of the cards are matched, the player with the most pairs wins.

You can play this game by yourself, too. Keep track of how long it takes you to match all of the pairs. Then play again, and see if you can beat your time.

Fact: If you want to find an antonym, look in a thesaurus. You will see the abbreviation "ant" next to it. The "ant" stands for antonym.

Glossary

autoantonym—a word that has two meanings that are the opposite of each other

complementary antonyms—words that are either one thing or another

graded antonyms—words that show how opposites are related

prefix—a set of letters added to the beginning of a word that can change the word's meaning

relational antonym—a word that has no meaning without its opposite

suffix—a set of letters added to the end of a word that can change the word's meaning

synonym—a word that means the same as another

Index

To Learn More

At the Library

Cleary, Brian P. *Stop and Go, Yes and No: What Is an Antonym?* Minneapolis: Carolrhoda, 2006.

Heinrichs, Ann. *Synonyms and Antonyms.* Chanhassen, Minn.: Child's World, 2006.

Pittau, Francisco. *Elephant Elephant: A Book of Opposites.* New York: Harry N. Abrams, 2001.

On the Web

FactHound offers a safe, fun way to find Web sites related to this book. All of the sites on FactHound have been researched by our staff.

1. Visit www.facthound.com
2. Type in this special code: 1404823840
3. Click on the FETCH IT button.

Your trusty FactHound will fetch the best sites for you!

Look for all of the books in the Word Fun series:

If You Were a Conjunction

If You Were a Homonym or a Homophone

If You Were a Noun

If You Were a Palindrome

If You Were a Preposition

If You Were a Pronoun

If You Were a Synonym

If You Were a Verb

If You Were an Adjective

If You Were an Adverb

If You Were an Antonym

If You Were an Interjection